PROVING CHARISMATIC GIFTS HAVE CEASED

PETER MASTERS

SWORD & TROWEL
METROPOLITAN TABERNACLE
LONDON

PROVING CHARISMATIC GIFTS HAVE CEASED

This booklet edition 2017

SWORD & TROWEL
Metropolitan Tabernacle
Elephant & Castle
London SE1 6SD

ISBN 978 1 899046 40 9

Cover design by Andrew Owen

Printed by Stephens & George, Merthyr Tydfil, UK

Proving Charismatic Gifts have Ceased

DOES THE BIBLE teach definitively that the charismatic gifts have ceased? Can cessationism (the view that they have ended) be proved? Some say that the cessation of the gifts cannot be conclusively proved from Scripture. We believe, however, that the ceasing of revelatory and sign-gifts in the time of the apostles is very plainly taught in God's Word, so plainly, in fact, that the opposite view has only seriously appeared in the last 100 years or so.

The term *cessationism* comes from the great 17th-century confessions of faith, such as the Westminster and Baptist confessions. These both use the same word. Speaking about how God has revealed his will and committed it to the Scriptures, the confessions say, 'former ways of God's revealing his will unto his people being now *ceased*'. This word does not actually come from the Bible, but the doctrine does.

Not only has revelation been completed and ceased, but so have the signs that revelation is in progress. Here is a brief summary of six biblical proofs that the revelatory gifts have ceased (visions, words of knowledge, words of wisdom, and prophecies), and also the sign-gifts (healings and speaking in tongues). God still heals, of course, but in answer to prayer, and not through the hands of a gifted healer.

The controversial passage of *1 Corinthians 13.8-10* will not be used in this booklet to prove the ending of the gifts. We will refer only to passages which we believe to be conclusive.

1. Not since the apostles

The first proof for the ending of revelatory and sign-gifts is that healings and wonders could only be done by apostles, and were their special authenticating signs. This is proved in *2 Corinthians 12.12* where Paul says: 'Truly the signs of an apostle were wrought among you in all patience, in signs, and wonders, and mighty deeds.'

There were some people in the church at Corinth who challenged Paul's apostleship. To defend himself he draws attention to his gift of healing and of working other miraculous signs, stating that only the apostles could do such things. An apostle was someone who had accompanied the Lord, seen him after his resurrection, and been personally commissioned by him. As a special witness of the resurrection he was given power to heal. He was also a person who would be shown 'all truth' by the Holy Spirit *(John 14.26* and *16.13)*, and would either write or endorse inspired Scripture.

Believers would need to know who the true apostles were in order to respect their unique authority. They would know them by their healings and other signs. People who did not belong to the band of apostles (which included just two named non-apostles) could not do these things. If they had been able to do them, then no one would have been certain who were true apostles. In *Acts 2.43* and *5.12* it is again made clear that all the miracles were performed 'by the hands of the apostles'. This was exclusively *their* sign. Also, in *Hebrews 2.3-4* the healing gifts are firmly linked only to the apostles – 'How shall we escape, if we neglect so great salvation; which at the first began to be spoken by the Lord, and was confirmed unto us by them that heard him; God also bearing them witness, both with signs and wonders, and with divers miracles, and gifts of the Holy Ghost, according to his own will?'

Paul was an apostle by virtue of having seen the risen Lord, and having been directly commissioned by him. His lack of training by Christ was made good by his receiving special and unique revelations. He states that he was 'one born out of due time' *(1 Corinthians 15.8)*, indicating that he was the only apostle outside the original band and therefore the last apostle. (Modern claims to apostleship do not match the biblical qualifications and are improper and wrong.)

When people say that the ceasing of sign-gifts cannot be proved from Scripture, they forget that the book of *Acts* says specifically that healings and other wonders were exclusive to the apostles, who have now passed away.

When the churches had grown and multiplied Peter went to Lydda, and then Joppa, famously healing Æneas and raising Dorcas from the dead. Entire communities were astonished, because none of the other believers in such places could do these things. When a lad fell out of a window in Troas, there was only one person present who could raise him up, and that was Paul. The charismatic idea that healings were performed by numerous Christians is simply not to be found in the New Testament. Only the apostles are recorded as having healed, together with just two of the men ordained by them as deacons, who clearly worked very closely with them, and may be regarded as their special representatives, namely Stephen and Philip. It is possible, but by no means certain, that Barnabas also healed while he worked alongside the apostle Paul.

The only time someone outside this group performed a healing was when the Lord told Ananias to heal Paul. There is no other healing apart from these in the early church. The Pentecostal-charismatic idea that healings took place constantly by Christians at large is not taught in the Bible. Thus the infallible record of Scripture shows the entire charismatic approach to healing to be a mistake based on a myth. The record proves that the healings and mighty deeds were restricted to a class of people who have passed away.

2. The temporary purpose of tongues

The second proof that sign-gifts have ceased is about tongues-speaking. It is the biblical statement that tongues-speaking was given by God specifically as a sign for Jews, signalling to them that the new era of Messiah had arrived.

In *1 Corinthians 14.21-22* Paul says,

> **'In the law it is written, With men of other tongues and other lips will I speak unto this people; and yet for all that will they not hear me, saith the Lord. Wherefore tongues are for a sign, not to them that believe, but to them that believe not.'**

In other words, the gift of tongues was a miraculous proof to Jews who were resistant to believing in Christ, that the new age and a new church order had arrived. It was not for the benefit of Jews who had come to believe, but a sign of promise and warning to those who did not believe. It was not intended for Gentiles, but Jews.

Paul quoted from *Isaiah 28.11*, a chapter in which Isaiah prophesies Christ's coming. As a sign to Jews, Isaiah says Jewish people will be addressed by those with 'stammering lips and another tongue'. Gentile languages will challenge them, a most belittling experience for Jewish people. At the same time it was a sign that the Messianic age would bring Gentiles into the church, and the Gospel would be preached in other languages.

This would be a mark of the new age when God would pull down the flag of the Jewish church, and run up the flag of the Jewish-Gentile church of Jesus Christ. Unbelieving Jews, who resisted Christ and clung to the skirts of Moses, would find the Word of God being preached to them in barbarian, Gentile languages. All this came to pass, beginning on the day of Pentecost. The Jews were duly called and warned, but tongues are not mentioned outside the *Acts of the Apostles* and *1 Corinthians 12-14*, showing that they had accomplished their purpose of warning the Jews that the new era had arrived.

This announcing of the church age was accomplished while the apostles lived, and the sign has been withdrawn. What passes for tongues-speaking today is not done in the presence of doubting Jews, and has nothing to do with the sign of the New Testament. The sign that the church age has come has served its purpose, and been surpassed by the reality. The Gospel is now preached in virtually every language in the world, and the sign that this would happen is long extinct. The purpose of tongues (according to *1 Corinthians 14,* quoted above) has been fulfilled, proving their discontinuation.

3. Tongues were real languages

The third proof of the cessation of the sign-gifts adds to the second, and it is this – that a gift of *real* languages was given on the day of Pentecost (and for a while afterwards), which has never been seen since that time. It should be obvious to us that the miraculous languages of the books of *Acts* and *1 Corinthians* have never been credibly reported as having occurred since those days. Tongues-speaking of modern times is never any known human language, but only disjointed speech, without meaning. Nothing miraculous happens. In New Testament times the tongues-speaker was given by the Spirit the ability to speak in a real language which he had never learned, and people who had grown up with him were astonished.

On the day of Pentecost many Jews who lived in foreign regions heard their own languages spoken, and attested the genuineness of the speakers. For a time after Pentecost the Spirit gave the miraculous gift of understanding to interpreters so that the authenticity of the languages could be proved. As far as we know nothing like this has been seen since Bible times.

Today those who advocate tongues-speaking point to *1 Corinthians 13.1* where Paul, speaking hypothetically, says that even if he spoke an *angelic* tongue, without love, it would amount to nothing. Desperately looking for a text, charismatic teachers take Paul's words as a justification for ecstatic, non-linguistic tongues, but it is plain to any thinking person that this is a serious misuse of the verse.

By describing literal languages, the Bible effectively tells us that these gifts have been withdrawn. They do not appear to have happened at any time in history, anywhere in the world, since the very early days of the church. What happens today is that people (who may be sincere Christians), in their desire to do what their leaders insist is right, seek to give utterance outside the rules of speech. However, they do not speak real languages, or even understand what they are saying. The cessation of the gifts is clearly taught in Scripture, by virtue of the fact that the very precise description of real languages given in Scripture cannot be applied to anything that has taken place since.*

Since Bible times we have had glorious events of reformation and mighty revivals, when the Spirit of God has been pleased to work in exceptional power. Yet we have not one reported or recorded claim of anyone speaking a real language they had never learned. This is certain proof that the gift of biblical tongues has ceased.

4. No instructions to appoint prophets

The fourth proof for the cessation of the sign-gifts is this: there are no New Testament instructions about appointing apostles, prophets, healers, or anything of the kind. This is a matter of tremendous significance, because God has given a detailed pattern for the church in the New Testament. It is true that some Christians do not believe that the Bible provides a blueprint for the church, but most people who are of baptistic, Bible-believing persuasion do.

The apostle Paul commands us repeatedly to be the most careful imitators of him in our church polity and conduct, and the pastoral epistles set out how we should behave and function in the church

---

* The unauthentic tongues-speakers of today do not even attempt to follow the Bible's rules for the exercising of the gift in those days – that no more than two or three at most should speak in any service *(1 Corinthians 14.27)*.

of God. We have instructions that most carefully set out how to select preaching and ruling elders and deacons, but no instructions about the appointment of apostles (because they were not to be perpetuated), or on how to recognise or accredit a prophet (because revelatory gifts ended with the completion of the Bible). Nor are there instructions about appointing healers.

This is not merely an argument from silence, but a proof that these offices and functions were not to continue. The instructions for all matters of church organisation are complete and detailed and all-sufficient for the church until Christ comes again. We disobey God's perfect pattern if we make appointments in the church that he has not prescribed and commanded. We disobey Scripture.

How can it be said that there is no certain scriptural proof that the gifts have ceased, when the pattern for the church gives no instructions for the continuation of inspired spokesmen and sign-workers? This is conclusive proof of cessation – unless we do not hold to the sufficiency of Scripture, and do not believe that God has given a pattern for his church.

5. Revelation is now complete

The fifth proof of the cessation of the revelatory and sign-gifts is that the Bible plainly teaches that revelation is now complete. There can be no new revelation after the time of the apostles. We have already noted that in *John 14.26* and in *John 16.13* the Lord Jesus Christ says twice to the disciples that the Holy Spirit, when he comes, will lead *them* into *all* Truth. They would be the authors of New Testament books, and the *authenticators* of inspired New Testament books not from their own pens. Soon *all* the Truth would be revealed, and after the apostolic era there would be no more revelation of Scripture. The Word would be complete.

How glad we are of that! What a state we would be in if people could pop up here, there and everywhere (as they do in the charismatic world) giving us new revelations. Who would know what was right, and what was true? But the Scripture is the final yardstick for everything, being complete and perfect, sufficient and trustworthy.

Jude was able to speak about the faith which was 'once delivered unto the saints'. His epistle was written possibly 25 years before the final book of the Bible, but late enough for all the main doctrines and church instructions to have been revealed. At this late stage of revelation he speaks of the faith *once* delivered, or better, *once for all* delivered. It was virtually completed; soon (from Jude's standpoint) there would be no more revelation.

The closing verses of the Bible warn that nothing must be added or taken from the words of the book of *Revelation*, but this clearly applies to the whole Bible, not just the last book. We know this because the warning closely echoes the one given by Moses in the first book of the Bible (the first five were originally one book), namely *Deuteronomy 4.2*, 'Ye shall not add unto the word which I command you, neither shall ye diminish aught from it' (words repeated by Moses in *Deuteronomy 12.32*).

The completion of revelation is also proved by the fact that apostles and prophets are described as the *foundation* stage of the church. In *Ephesians 2.20* the church is described as being – 'built upon the foundation of the apostles and prophets *[that is – New Testament prophets]*, Jesus Christ himself being the chief corner stone'. A foundation is something completed and stable, while the building continues to be constructed.

What about Joel's prophecy, quoted by Peter on the day of Pentecost, saying that when the Spirit is poured out, all believers, male, female, old and young will prophesy? Is it not implied that this will go on literally until the Lord's return? No, because our understanding of this prophecy must agree with the unassailable teaching of the Bible that revelation was soon completed, and then ceased.

It is this completed revelation (especially the Gospel) that will be the witness of believers of all ages, male and female, through all the world, until the end. Believers will continue to see visions and dream dreams in the sense that they embrace, reflect upon, and proclaim the infallible visions and dreams given to them in the Bible. They will not 'prophesy' in the sense of receiving new revelation. They will also dream dreams of Gospel plans and conquests. In this sense the prophecy of Joel is still being fulfilled. The extraordinary manifestations such as tongues had clearly vanished by the time Peter wrote his two epistles (30-35 years later), for he gives no hint whatsoever that these features of the early scene were still operating.

As revelation was completed in the time of the apostles, we see that the task of apostles and prophets is over. And if the gifts of revelation are ended, then so are the authenticating signs of inspired penmen. We remember how Paul said, 'Truly the signs of an apostle were wrought among you in…signs, and wonders, and mighty deeds' *(2 Corinthians 12.12)*.

How can it be said that there is no biblical proof of the withdrawal of revelatory gifts (and their confirming signs) when Scripture emphatically says that all revelation has been completed, like a foundation, at the beginning of the church age?

6. Scripture witnesses the end of gifts

The sixth proof of the ending of the sign-gifts is that Scripture shows that they were in the process of being withdrawn at that very time. Paul, for example, who possessed apostolic power to do signs and wonders and mighty deeds, could not, in the course of time, heal Timothy or Trophimus or Epaphroditus.

We also see the withdrawing of the healing gifts in *James 5*, where James gives instructions about praying for the sick, and how the elders may lay hands upon the bedridden. It is obvious in this passage that there is no gifted healer in sight, only elders who pray. Anointing is mentioned, but the Greek term for religious anointing is not used. The Greek uses a very practical word that means 'rub down' with oil, more like a remedy for bedsores. James effectively says, 'Don't be so heavenly-minded that you are of no earthly use, but take some physical relief for the suffering person.' What matters most is prayer. It is certain in the instructions of James that no gifted healer is brought in to command healing, or to give a healing touch. The laying on of hands of ordinary elders is a symbolic act, communicating the church's love, care and responsibility.

The main point for us in this booklet is that there is no one possessing personal power to heal in *James 5*. Healing is by God in answer to prayer, there being four distinct exhortations to pray. The ongoing stance of the church is seen as praying for healing, yet remembering that some are called to live as 'an example of suffering affliction, and of patience' *(James 5.10)*. The fact that James does not mention healing gifts shows unmistakably that the possession of healing power was withdrawn quite early in the course of the apostolic era.

Would a neutral reader assume Bible gifts were for every age?

It has been suggested that if a new convert with no experience of church life were shut in a room with a Bible, it would never occur to that person that the charismatic gifts had ceased. The opposite is true. There are many people (we know some) who come from other faiths who have been converted to Christ by private Bible reading, and subsequently found their way into a church. From the Bible alone they received no expectation of a charismatic scene.

Much more frequently – increasingly so as time passes – believers leave charismatic churches having realised that what takes place there is not what they find in the Bible. On reading *Acts* carefully, they discover that only the apostolic band healed, and feel they have been misled by the Pentecostal/charismatic notion that numerous people did so.

Some wonder what the original significance or purpose of tongues was, and when they learn from Paul that they were specifically for Jews, they again feel misled by their teachers. They also feel mis-taught when it becomes obvious that tongues were real languages, a vastly more miraculous matter than incomprehensible sounds.

Then, as soon as these believers appreciate the importance of the scriptural pattern for the church, the question arises in their minds – 'Where are the Bible's instructions for appointing apostles, prophets and healers today?' They find there are none, and become even more critical of the teaching they have received.

Then the question of the authority and sufficiency of Scripture intrudes, and they think, 'Is not revelation complete? How, then, can modern prophecies be valid and inspired?' It becomes obvious that all the 'authoritative' prophecies they have heard are a great mistake, and a delusion. Many thinking believers see for themselves that to charismatic people, Scripture is second in importance to human imagination and mysterious experiences.

Finally, the more these friends study the Word, the more they see the evidence that the signs disappeared soon after their spectacular initial outpouring.

None of this means that the Lord does not move his people to remember duties or truths, or urge them to do certain things, or warn them of imminent dangers. These are divine intimations, not revelations or gifts.

In the history of the church, there are recorded instances of people having an intimation from God about some threatening event or person, but these are never revelations of doctrine. We find such things in times of severe persecution. For instance, up until Perestroika in Russia, we heard of very credible instances when God's key servants were wonderfully delivered from arrest because the Lord impressed on someone not to go to some particular place. It was later discovered that a KGB-police ambush lay in wait for them. However, no recipient of such an intimation was given a regular gift, and certainly not an authoritative revelation of doctrinal truth. God can do all kinds of things to deliver and bless his people, but this is not in any way the reappearance of apostolic or prophetic gifts bestowed on individuals.

The damage of charismatic teaching

Many charismatics are coming to see the enormous gap between the Bible and what they have been taught. Such doubters are often troubled by the fact that huge numbers of Catholics, who depend on Mary, the Mass, and works for salvation, are also able to speak in tongues and prophesy. Such Catholics worship in exactly the same way as charismatic Protestants.

Charismatic doubters may also hear that non-Christian cults also speak in tongues. You do not need to be a saved Christian to speak in charismatic-style tongues, because it is not a true gift of the Spirit.

There are many sincere Christians in the charismatic movement, but we believe that the attempt to revive revelatory and sign-gifts is a very harmful mistake. We can see the harm in the emergence of huge sections of the movement in which the Gospel has virtually disappeared, buried under unbiblical extravagances.

There are large charismatic groups that now deny the penal substitution of Christ, and some even deny the Trinity. (One of the world's most famous charismatic preachers and authors denies the doctrine of the Trinity.) Worldly entertainment-style music dominates charismatic churches, even music of the most extreme and godless kind. The theatrical antics of money-grabbing charismatic leaders may be seen at any time on religious TV, and the prosperity-gospel heresy is seemingly everywhere.

Numerous charlatans and rogues have built large followings, carrying out their supposed 'healings' at venues throughout the world. Even music-hall fortune-telling techniques are being presented as spiritual wonders, in once respected churches.

The powerful current that constantly propels the charismatic constituency further and further from the Bible is evidence of a serious fundamental error, namely, the idea that the revelatory and sign-gifts are for all time. To experience them involves a twofold mistake: firstly, the downscaling of the gifts to something non-miraculous (eg: turning real languages into non-linguistic utterances); and secondly, the downgrading of Scripture, which must bow to imagined experiences of dreams, visions, 'words from the Lord', and similar revelations.

There is harm done also to individual Christians whose faith is greatly diverted from the Lord and his Word, to phenomena and sensations. We sincerely pray that God will deliver those who are his true children from the accumulating harm of this wildly mistaken departure from Scripture.

Other books on this subject by Dr Masters

This brief digest of the reasons why the gifts have ceased cannot deal with all the queries readers may raise. A fuller presentation, with a large answers-to-questions section is provided in the author's book, *The Charismatic Illusion.* Another title, *The Healing Epidemic,* deals with the scriptural teaching on healing and also demonstrates the fallacy of modern demon occupation. A further book by the author – *Only One Baptism of the Holy Spirit* – shows that the baptism of the Spirit, in Scripture, is simultaneous with conversion.

Sermons of Dr Masters, audio or video,
may be downloaded or viewed free of charge on the
website of the Metropolitan Tabernacle:
www.metropolitantabernacle.org

The Charismatic Illusion

Peter Masters & John C Whitcomb

100 pages, paperback, Wakeman Trust, ISBN 978 1 908919 70 0

Now with more answers to questions asked by people investigating the arguments, this veteran book contends for the biblical position on the gifts that prevailed for nearly 2,000 years before the charismatic movement came along.

Here is the dynamic teaching of the Spirit that sustained true churches and believers through dark and bright years of history, through the Reformation, through the Puritan era, through the time of great Confessions of Faith, through repeated awakenings and revivals, and through the worldwide growth of the modern missionary movement.

Here is the case for authentic, biblical, spiritual life.

The Healing Epidemic

Peter Masters

143 pages, paperback, Wakeman Trust, ISBN 978 1 908919 24 3

Dr Masters here answers the arguments used by healers in support of their methods. He explains Bible teaching on what demons can and cannot do, and how *James 5* should be implemented in churches today. He also proves that the conscious mind should always be switched on for spiritual activities. Included is a brilliant assessment of miraculous healing by a leading British medical professor.

Only One Baptism of the Holy Spirit

Peter Masters

86 pages, paperback, Wakeman Trust, ISBN 978 1 908919 78 6

Young Christians these days are confronted by much confusion on the teaching of the Holy Spirit and how he baptises, fills and anoints God's people. Contradictory statements and clashing ideas flow from a new generation of anecdotal-style books.

When is the believer baptised with the Spirit, and what does it amount to? Is there a second baptism? How exactly does the Spirit witness with our spirit? How does assurance come? Is the believer to struggle against sin, or does the Lord fight the battle for him? What is the filling of the Spirit? Clear answers are given to all such questions, with 'proof texts'.